ABOUT THE AUTHOR

Nicki Heinen was born in Germany and moved to the UK aged 6. She studied English at Girton College, Cambridge University, where she won the Barbara Wrigley Prize for Poetry. She completed an MA in Creative and Life Writing at Goldsmiths College in 2012, with distinction. Her work has been published in a variety of print and on-line magazines and anthologies, including *Magma*, and Bloodaxe's *Staying Human Anthology*. She was shortlisted for the Pat Kavanagh Prize and was commended in the Winchester Poetry Prize 2018 and 2020. She founded and hosts Words & Jazz, a spoken word and music night, at the Vortex Jazz Café, London, and the Words & Art online series. Her pamphlet *Itch* was launched with Eyewear Press in May 2017 and it was a London Review Bookshop book of the year. *There May Not Be A Reason Why* is her debut collection. She lives in North London.

Website: http://nickiheinen.com/
Twitter: @nickiheinen
Instagram: @nickiheinen

Nicki Heinen

There May Not Be a Reason Why

VERVE
POETRY PRESS
BIRMINGHAM

PUBLISHED BY VERVE POETRY PRESS
https://vervepoetrypress.com
mail@vervepoetrypress.com

All rights reserved
© 2022 Nicki Heinen

The right of Nicki Heinen to be identified as author of this work has been asserted in accordance with section 77 of the Copyright, Designs and Patents Act 1988.

No part of this work may be reproduced, stored or transmitted in any form or by any means, graphic, electronic, recorded or mechanical, without the prior written permission of the publisher.

FIRST PUBLISHED JAN 2022

Printed and bound in the UK
by Imprint Digital, Exeter

ISBN: 978-1-912565-65-8

For Mum and Dad

CONTENTS

Summer at St Pancras Hospital	11
The Houseplant Has Come Alive	12
Rosewood Ward	13
Chaconnes	14
Solent Ward	15
#MeToo	17
The Fashionista Moths of Highgate	18
Movie Night on Isis Ward	19
Don't Obsess Over Things You Can't Control	20
There May Not be a Reason Why	21
Self	22
Sinkhole	23
Marrakesh / The Riad is Burning	24
Customise the Apocalypse	25
La Gironde	26
There may be another one of me	27
Inferno at Addenbrookes	29
Being Twelve	31
Functioning	32
Missive	34
Itch / Midnight on Ward S4	35
14 ways of looking at the colour white	36

Interludes	37
Quarantine in a flat at the cradle of the station	39
Aftershave	40
Blues / Everyone wants me to be well	44
Fire-eating in Waterloo	45
Pink	46
The Night Before	47
Lace	48
The Abandoned	50
To an Ex-Lover	51
Evolution	52
The Red Dress	53
Purple and Red	54
Three Short Poems for Music	55
Snowstorm	57
The Mouth of the River Grief	58
Melancholia	59
Walk with my Father	60
The Crows at Chatressac	61
Hell's Angels	63
The Cat King	64
Lay All Your Love on Me	66
Young	67
Lebowski	68
Birthday on Rosewood Ward	70
Journeying North	71

'*...be patient towards all that is unresolved in your heart and try to love* the questions themselves *like locked rooms, like books written in a foreign tongue.*'

Rainer Maria Rilke *Letters to a Young Poet*

'*at this party nobody cries. at this party nobody is bored or afraid...a banner in the sky:* it doesn't matter it doesn't matter it doesn't matter that you feel this way.'

Sophie Robinson *Rabbit*

There May Not Be a Reason Why

Summer at St Pancras Hospital

You could never imagine it: a California sun bleeding down on the rotting plaster, the cracked tiles erupting weeds, a summer gone bad in the crater of today, yesterday, tomorrow, every day the same but for the occasional bath. The two trees behind the barbed-wire-topped wall have birthed leaves, I watch the jigsawed green as I smoke. Claire is doing star jumps in Lycra, and at 12 a nurse comes out with a box of nail varnishes. We congregate like nuns around the rainbowed box and pounce for the right colour. Cranberry reds, poison purple, swimming pool turquoise, gold with iridescent specks. It's a bomb in a fruit shop. The heat swells my toes and the rat in the corner snuffles trash. The sun is so high it ain't never coming down.

The Houseplant Has Come Alive

all you need to know about
my pain is that
the other side of the universe is
each of us
light wind freckling our faces
morsel of lobster-in-cream
look at the sun and the rocks
the sea the sea the sea

The world tilting
at the flick of acrylic paint
blocked yellows shine like

coral fish shuttering in blue
and the houseplant has come alive
but it's not what you think

Rosewood Ward

on the floor a sea of glitter
which I couldn't taste
on the walls, dirt
the bed – narrow and light –
a sheet, white with NHS monogram
and a pinky-pearl blanket
with soft insidious hairs
the curtain frayed, bluebell-smash colour

and on one damp wall was a cracked mirror
reflecting hospital greys
the door didn't lock

but I couldn't get out –
the radio played all night, songs of cornfields
and a choir of monks from Bulgaria

Chaconnes

i /
juice it / hang it to dry
splinter of lemon / drop of sun
the yolk of a good day / the bleed of the blue
when you spring up / you leave it to honeysuckle

ii /
new shoes by the bed / stepping light in fur
morning 2pm / weak sunlight a patch on the floor
dipped in almond milk / chocolate curls
oh but when the clock strikes 10pm/ duvet folded around a thick waist
it is not a desperate situation / it is the best compromise

iii /
there's room for one in my bed / and the cat king
your small frame gone / no more you shaped hole
I'm through with you / shout it from the balcony
no longer sad / the beginning of a new lifetime

iv /
smoke fuels smoke / inhale like a chimp grooming
scent of tobacco / hair dripping
it is a small pleasure / lungs fighting
a five minute high / the energy of a toddler
green shoots in the earth / feel like singing

Solent Ward

The nurse says nothing as
he follows me, keeping the length of two corpses
behind me. I see him only out of the corner
of my eye. He comes in to my room
pushes the door behind him, it shuts
with a papery click

Shhh
he says, as he puts a finger to his lips. He is not much taller
than me, greasy, with a slipped face and stubble
He puts a hand on each of my arms
steadies me in case I run
and leans in, smelling of hand sanitiser. Kisses me
long and hard, making sure I kiss back.
He moves his hands to my breasts and feels around slowly.
Then he leaves, closing the thin door.

I peel off my gold top and put it in the bin
sit in my bra for a minute. Then I put on a sweatshirt
and retch over the sink
wipe my mouth clean of smeared lipstick
with the blue and white NHS towel, and push open the door.
Walk to the office round the corridor
but he's got there first.

He is talking to a female nurse. She is round
with a silver brooch on her cardigan. Her hair is peppery grey
    and wispy.

I take her out of the room
and tell her what has happened. He is inside typing
a report about me on the desktop computer. I can see my name
at the top.

She puts on a sympathy face; the corners of her mouth turn down.
I hear her say
Nicki, dear, you're not well.
Nobody here would harm you.
Why don't you go to your room and have a little lie down.

#MeToo

this skin dries bloodless, underneath a ghost slip scratches pale-blue
feather in my mouth turns liquid like tide-pods exploding
the sun is absent, a carnation wilts on the grave, a shadow not falling
no crater so deep as the hole in my mind, filled with all the things I said
all the things you took, all the things undone
furniture of the bipolar kingdom, stuffed full of dust-mites
burrowing in like spun tops
is it not an exercise set for the next time?
no, it's not
it's this moment in which I stand
a woman enfettered
stand with feather in mouth
my blood on your lips, your face etched in the winter air
my head splintering, a silent grenade

The Fashionista Moths of Highgate

Black-eared, white-winged, they edge in silently
frequencies unheard, they signal
each to each a whisper like whipped cream
each to each desirous of cloth, each to each nattily naked.

Silk slips a luncheon of kings
cashmere a royal buffet

polyester cardigan untouched.

Come to me you Highgate moths
and I will cover myself in velvet,
wings fluttering like cassette-tape in the wind
your tiny antennae pricking towards the virgin wool,
smother me in cotton and leave me blind as a blank book.

You come to destroy and
I can understand that.

Movie Night on Isis Ward

Oh if only you would shut the door! She says. If only you would come in and sit on the sofa like a calm person. How is all this smoking of cigarettes and running about the yard going to help you?

When can I go home? I say I can't stand being here and alone and you think I'm not right in the head. I'm perfectly alright, I just know I'm the Messiah. I come inside and sit on the sofa, then get up again and go and pour myself a glass of Coke as befits the Messiah. Lily the anorexic asks me for an egg cupful of Coke. *Cheers* she says, and we take a sip. Lynsy sits on a chair with broken arms. She says nothing. The wind comes in through the cracks in the French doors and I wish, again, that I was at home. *Movie night,* She says, but we say nothing. I reach into my pocket for my packet and get up again. *I'm going for a smoke* I say, and pull my coat around me.

Don't Obsess Over Things You Can't Control

The poppy in the garden will
die before the autumn's over
and I'm not OK with that fact.
Neither is it right or proper
that I myself am finite as
poppies fading in the cold wind.
Is it the end yet? Put your red
dress on and dance the winter in.

There May Not be a Reason Why

I grab fistfuls of quiet magnolia
gun down the squad of thought police
camped outside my kitchen door

it may not be a clever idea
to utter kitkat noise
in the bedroom naked

while the Schadenfreude drips from my wrists

but the dumb giraffe in my belly
is dancing

I put my hands into
the steel pail of soaked raspberries
just to feel the blood
dab the juice on my breasts

and yes you are in my thoughts
as you sometimes are

Self

Nothing hurts like a dead moth

Sinkhole

Gutting abstraction takes
its toll. Two cigarettes and I'm yours
It's the long-shaded part of the day
and the city birds are tweeting
a large gin infused with blueberries
sink into the foundations of this
sand-pooled house
sucked down by smoke and water
gonna swim in a pool the colour of lorazepam
just as soon as I get out of here
the bulldozers come to shatter this
vitreous building to the ground
nothing is left but banks and Starbucks paper-
cups to bite into
and the mayflower becomes a moon
the sun has sunk
and if I ever knew a cure, I've
lost it now

Marrakesh / The Riad is Burning

The desert is dry as skin
the ground is
crisp-nut brown
sometimes reddish blood

I run a fingernail to trace a line
it snags on the sun
blanched bushes punctuate the horizon
my eyes are filmy with looking

you have a red mouth
which spits seeds
they grow in the desert

your hot breath blooms

toes grow lichen and moss
a garden in gold
at night you snake into something
sinful and drear

you chase giants till they fall down dead
you pierce the shell of an egg
bleed it by blowing till it's hollow
blow till it daren't crack
you run and run
until the sun drowns in the sand
turning cold

Customise the Apocalypse

with personal number plates
W3'R3 ALL GO1NG 2 D1E
in one way or another
it's the method in the madness
hear the soldier cry
in the deserted football pitch
the forest is shrinking like
wrapped chicken in the microwave
the hustle, oh the hustle
the rustle of crack-tin foil
the dreary din of the ward
horror, horror, I've lived through it all
and in the end, it becomes a dog treat on the nose
bring it on, king, because on the last day
we will all be one

La Gironde

I'm searching wildly
for a path I can call my own, along deadbeat streets –
white into oil-spill into stop-sign into rain –
grey falling over everything like a spotted trout sinking.

Step to the door
that opens on the hair of the moon,
swing from the rafters humming a bitter tune –
a bitter little tune

I have nothing to say
when I look into the eyes of the moon
as she watches me hesitate by the cliff edge

la lune ne garde aucune rancune
but she narrows her salty eyes and tuts – I can see it
She whispers I'm childish
for these translucent dreams
of hidden oceans –
it is only in dreams you taste saltwater
kiss the heroine

The night is wearing its heat tight –
close-cropped like topiary
but it is cold across the universe,
I feel it

There may be another one of me

a shadow,
sitting in a pool of silver light across the bay,
cross-universe, another one of me cross-legged,
sitting listening and gazing quietly back.

Shadow?
Hair pricks on my neck.
The sea sucks at the cliffs,
I know you're there.

Cloud arched like a leopard's back,
moon pushing silver on a tiled floor.
Tar-sprinkled sky.

What does it matter, when there is silver on the floor?
One star...two stars...three...

The moon makes a white skin across the water,
I'll run to get to you,
perhaps before daybreak we'll meet.

I'd like you, I suppose,
because I'm getting older and I have more to regret.

I regret the silvery street made for me by the moon,
because I'm at the cliff edge and I see nothing stopping me
from jumping to meet you.
When we meet you will close your eyes
and I'll see the feathered darkness of your eyelids

as you put your hand on mine.
I'll close my lashes and see crimson,
I'll feel your breath on my arm.

Our eyes will meet
as the clouds
join our feet.

We'll drink black coffee
and sit cross-legged,
till the sun warms us.

You will be more
beautiful than I imagined,
more fragile.
If I put my hand through yours it will break.

Lost years will flash over your face like logo-rhythms,
your toes will curl at the sight of the sun.

Go ahead
You'll whisper,
Live.

Inferno at Addenbrookes

The hospital I live in is a corrupt palace
as bloody as a monthly jab.

I can't speak for laughing,
stretched spasm
takes me to the lip of the canyon.

I look down on a house of cards,
dying inside but laughing laughing
till the beat in my chest snaps
and my head rocks.

I hear sirens and birdsong, they sound like signals from outer-space.
I start dancing to pop, dancing with Chrissie who is dark and
    frightening,
Her hair is short, she bellows at me shuffling out of time.
I sit on the exercise bike in men's pyjamas with nothing underneath,
worried the flies will fall open and Nurse Allah-cum-Salaam will see.
I have no idea who I am and the rain beats so that the glass shakes.

Lock-up, lock-in, lock-tight.
I never knew freedom till it was gone,
Never tasted liberty till
I was given 20 minutes a day.
Never understood why air is so fresh till I had only a courtyard for it.
Hysterics, broken glass, psychosis.

I refuse to eat slop,
smash the vending machine for crisps.

Nasty nurse is not happy with me
for my repeated requests
Are you the Devil? Am I in Hell?
The bathroom smells of shit,
there's some smeared on the bath rail.

Greasy hair in braids,
I start to smell
of this institution.

A Coke can is my ash tray.

Locked in my room all night
and all day.

Puff puff
I'm not hurt,
though I bang on the door till my fist is red.

I stop eating anything but cheese sandwiches,
tell my psychiatrist everything tastes of piss.
He says this is an unusual symptom.
From the high windows flanking the long corridor
I can see a chimney pumping smoke from the distance.
Dead bodies are burnt there, this is a camp.
Turkish delight on my tongue
sticks like glue.
When the rain stops it's midnight and the lights are out.
The chimney's still smoking.

Being Twelve

Crisp snow in April
grinning down ankles stiff as spaghetti
and that band you love playing in your ear
Oui j'adore –
how many times you tried to find the cure
and it takes a bed-wetting rift to get there
onely as ... like stars but quiet inside
letting them talk and eating the language while it's hot

Functioning

I am having trouble stringing sentences together
she said

I am having trouble breathing
I am feeling very sad
she said

I am angry all the time, I am sad
she said

as she ate a forkful of mushroom and tomato spaghetti

I am due to see the doctor
she said

as she scooped up some mozzarella

Can the doctor cure me?
she said

as she sipped on a Diet Coke

I am afraid of solipsism
she said

as she popped an olive into her mouth

Can they cure that?
she said

her mum said
Yes

Missive

This is my dead letter
my notebook of sifted seeds
my kraken-spilly of ghost thoughts

In the middle of the night
when it is soft and
varnished as a boat's hull,
when the angels
and dogs have gone to sleep

I send you a grey gull to
lick feathers into your lovely eyes
I finger the ventricles of your
mended heart, stitch one button
to your mouth so you can
see again, so you see me again

Itch / Midnight on Ward S4

There's a little thing of black
flicks from glass-eye to mouth to heart –
fills me up.

No-one knows
how small my eye shrinks,
doctor can't help me.

Hearing radio noise
I shut my glass eye tight,
lock it out.

Night mouse
behind the sink
makes a scratch –
I itch it free.

Milk spills out of a cup

the leaves and the moon and the fence
reflect hush

I break codes with wallpaper.

What end
to the night-watch in this asylum
on this night and again on the next?

14 ways of looking at the colour white

Around you a necklace of teeth –
a thin plastic bag just emptied – to put it in
ripped feather – light wind
at the edge of the road – December
streetlamp blinking 5am
fog that gets in your nostrils
cracked china in the soil
roots growing there
while the piece-of-shit radiator rattles
eyes in the Old Master
aspirin – downed
sick dawn
bleached ink
page turned

Interludes

i /
under the earth is warm earth / breathe it
note of whisky / snail track / beetroot
the stars beggar the sky / a hummingbird blinks
tonight a cross word will be hanging in the air / the clouds stay
    away for fear
break the bread and swallow / if it doesn't taste sweet you're
    doing it wrong

ii /
taste the sour-sweetness of the long day / feel it swell
under sky of benefactress / undying atheist glory
I choose this / live with it / crave it
and when the tide turns / the seaweed will dry as salt
the whole earth is spinning / too fast to take a breath / too fast
    to survive

iii /
beneath every tooth / a hole
black wild / sucking the glass out of me
as delicate / as a bra-let
on a 17-year-old
kissing a boy / in the bed of night

iv /
crack of whip / horse leaps and whinnies
violets / on the tongue
at the bottom of the well / lies a skull
what I ask for / is not what I get
what I get / is more than I ask for

v /
you make me think / of whisky in space
the last drop / trickling down my throat
a pearl rolling down Scafell Pike
the stars / companions to sing to in broken French
oh god, it is not enough to be thankful / we must be brave too

Quarantine in a flat at the cradle of the station

Because the day is elastic and quiet, because Coca Cola sustains me, because my cat purrs and the sound astounds me, because everything is wrong, because there is no right way, because birds sing in the hollow of no trains moving, because I wouldn't get up, and I wouldn't get up, because now it's so late and the sun is going down, and my cat is still sleeping, because I have taken two sleeping pills at 6am because I still couldn't sleep, because now I can't get up, because my friends are silent and depressed, because there is ant poison on the floor, because my drying socks haven't been put away, because I hurt in my heart because I am partially cut up by nicotine, because the new way of living is no way of living, because apathy kills.

Aftershave

1: Kouros

voices mingle in the packed hall
we sing

later we lie

the stain on your bedsheets
a broken refrain

Have you slept with her yet

I watered your basil plant in the morning
when you had gone to work

left a note

where is it now

2: sea salt

you came from the ocean
and you were part of it

wind and spray made you

your delicate fingers

why did I not talk

why did you not talk

how was it ever so beautiful

apart, there were the dull letters
I read them and filed them away

but you spoke in ocean tongues
gave the rest to your sweaty body on mine

the caravan, shaking

the fires on the beach

the late guitar

and I did not see you as mine, ever

I did not see you

3: Hugo Boss

how to begin when there was no beginning
and a silent end

the years stuttered by

I can only imagine my suffering
I did not live it, lived beyond

there is no escape from a bully

only the years that glide by

presently under no circumstances to be repeated

it was a lush night, that first kiss a flower

but the rest I unthink

4: Chanel Pour l'Homme

I followed a man down the street
once, because he smelt of you

not knowing
was the hook

a bent arm, a sideways look
your first sushi, your first Thomas Ades

and then the night we didn't
I expected more

lived in the promise

of a poem that never arrived

5: Lacoste

just the scent of it

wild

unbounding from the core

a sniff, that crack erotica

just a tiny smell

enough to spread my legs
spread yours

enough to remind me
I once was adored

Blues / Everyone wants me to be well

I never wanted to be ill in the head, I never asked for it. I never said yes let's be mad, let's believe in stupid shit, let's get naked. I never looked in the mirror and said I'm beautiful, I never wanted to be heard, I never wanted to be seen. I never stared straight in the eyes of a frog, I never asked to be heartbroken. I never looked up a phone number in the yellow pages at a hospital and called it and said I've been abused. I never ordered pizza and put it in the bin. I never hugged a plushie at night, I never threw it away in the morning. I never put on lipstick to snare a council worker, I never misread the wording on a sweatshirt, I never asked to be mad.

Fire-eating in Waterloo

And in the damp spot beneath the stairs I placed the roses.
They burn yellow, gold, sunset-pink
the edges of each flower crumpling like broken skin.
It's a shame you'll never smell them.

The taste of oysters is sea-glue, melted crayon, hair-gel, semen,
the grit in each one an aborted pearl. Whitstable, Chatressac,
    Loch Fyne.
With a pearl on each earlobe, ripped tights, black bomber boots,
    I wait for my limo
on a thundery night in Clapton. Whisky in my left hand, a
    cigarette in the other.

Damp logs burn, hiss, offer a priceless stink,
newspaper huffs and spits, flames moving like molten glass,
the proofs of my ten-year novel, gone in two minutes and
    forty-three seconds,
I count the time. I feel a year younger with every page destroyed.

This is not an exercise in living, this is organ donation –
Feel the anguish and pronounce it dead.

Pink

I take it
feel it surge and stretch
under the tongue
taste salted caramel
suck the poison out
of the flower
texture like ridged rice-paper
like warm ice-cream
It grows and grows
till taste spills
and swills out
of my pink mouth

The Night Before

All the while he lay next to me
in his spandex briefs, dark red, with navy piping
and he didn't look at me

I was not able to think clearly, and very afraid
this was just after he called me baby for the last time
I fiddled with the ring on my finger
twisting and twisting it

And the cat sat at the end of the bed and I
tried to reach to stroke him
but instead of stroking him I said *so we're getting married and buying
    the flat still?*
and he said *yes...*

But the next day he packed a rucksack
and left to stay with his parents
and that was the last time I saw him

Lace

The shop is closeted within a 60s block and up three flights of concrete; we pass through an architect's office to get to it,
iMacs and cardboard models ablaze with the light slashing through the windows;
there are sixty white dresses on racks, a cabinet full of flowered head-dresses and then the veils –
everything in this shop hanging stiffly like pelts, like trophies. The dresses are delicate as origami,
ridden with studded pearls and flowers and flickering gems. Who knew that there were this many shades of white?
My head is heavy with last night's wine and I'm stepping into another life,
one that could have been mine, one that should have been mine, one that is not mine.

She picks five, and the assistant reaches up to close the wine-dark velvet curtain,
blocking the bride from view as the secret ritual plays out. I sit on the patterned chaise-longue,
not knowing what I should be feeling, not knowing if I will ever be able to feel again.

I keep sitting, waiting; a drowning fly in a cup of milk. I feel nauseous;
    I still hurt here in the chest
here where he belonged, here where I could tap with ringed finger
    less than a year ago,
knowing I had this – this love, this trust. A little year ago?
She comes out in her favourite, and looks like a rose-drop on the
    tongue, lace covering her body in a tattoo of dust,
the neck gathered with a delicate ruching so that her head emerges a
    golden phoenix, a whispering victor, a silent ending note.
I look at her whiteness and breathe in, out, blinded by the texture of
    silken spun roses on the hips,
I want to dive into her and pull my own lost love from deep inside
    her, pull in and get my own dress out.

The Abandoned

I imagine you in a glass box,
which I have kept secret and hidden.
It is rectangular and sits in the living room like a blood stain.
I polish it nightly, spraying with the brand that you prefer,
taking the kitchen towel in folds and smoothing the drops till
    its sides shine.
You look restful and safe.
While I sleep, you reach out and stroke my cheek.
It is better this, than to see the box empty,
my hands turning feathery with over-use and my hair growing
    greyer
in the mirror. The mirror shows me your shadow, soft as felt,
but when I ask it for a kiss it wisps away, a tower of ash
dissolving in the breeze.
I ask my lovers if they will say my name, gently, as you did;
they cannot. They take the mirror and hold it up to my face.
Look, they say, *you are alone.*

To an Ex-Lover

Oh your erect cock!
What's seen cannot be unseen

Addictive green cries
penetrate me

My body groaning with the weight
of the promises you made:

No town could bury them
there are no graveyards wide enough
no skip-dumps deep as your lying throat

Your promises are toxic as
a thousand rainbow-coloured bottle tops
on a white beach in the Indian Ocean
a Tennent's six-pack plastic around the head of a turtle

Oh your cock is a TV
showing the image of a lover
you
smiling in the arms of your beloved

I turn it off

Evolution

I have old bus tickets and a blue lighter in my pocket.
You look at me –
my face is an advert for loneliness
and I know that you will forget me when I say hello.

Your hands are weapons –
they make me feel breakable and alive.

The flames of the fire
fight – flicker – Plato's cave
(are shadows more beautiful?)
I am drunk.
You say to me -
    What are you doing here?

I wish I were not here.
I wish I were a photon in a far-flung galaxy
waiting for a black hole to engulf me so I can cease to exist –
like candy cigarettes
or the Bali tiger – though I guess that would still be here if it
    had a choice.

I am failing at evolution in ways that a tiger cannot
    comprehend.

The Red Dress

He bought it for me
after I'd got fined £50
for putting out my cigarette in the street

Foul taste in my mouth
but he said the dress suited me

Too tight
ruching down the bodice
and an asymmetrical neck

It made me feel like his property
which I loathed and loved

I wore it twice
shoved it to the back of the cupboard

Then found it five years
after he left me

Felt sick

Cried

Gave it to Oxfam

Purple and Red

after Mark Rothko

Snow on paper dampens my hair and eyelashes.
When I blink it dissolves.
Scratch n' sniff:
there is purple –

Oyster-shell box, red milk, silk kite-tail.

Red paints despair and quivers there.

Dance to it
the voice says in my head.
I can't.

Three Short Poems for Music

Three Fantasy Pieces by Robert Schumann

A box opens and out fly cut-glass buttons, lilac petals, a tiny red shoe, a cat's warm bed, small candles lit up in jewelled colours, a set of miniature books, leather bound, inked in grey, the song of a starling, a milk tooth, your first words: mama, elephant, my tissue-paper-wrapped heart, the touch of your lips like a feathered dress. All this, because the box is mine but I give it to you.

Three Romances by Clara Schumann

The fire burns and builds, it warms my dead hands till they spark – see? I have forgot what I was going to bury under the fig tree, it doesn't matter now, now that you're here and spring is coming fast, can you hear the birds hurrying? Their feet are kindling and their wings are petroleum, they fly on fire to the song of the seasons.

Songs without Words by Felix Mendelssohn

The clouds scud; up ahead a storm breaks, wasting the trees like the Black Death, raindrops cling to rose petals scattered on the ground and I remember, oh I remember when you plucked a lily from the pond and placed it behind my ear, I remember when we were nearly wed, when your feet tucked under mine for warmth in the iron bed – spring is brief, soon comes winter again with his ravaging. All is quickly lost.

Snowstorm

There is light breaking out from the queen's tomb
in a far-forgotten city where the cars' jaws eat bread crusts
fed by urchin children in velvet suits.
A gone land, sore threaded carpets made by moths on the palace
   floors,
a debt-ridden hungry place of hurricanes that pass by
devolved of power. Click-clack go the heels of the lawyers coming
to unseat the throne, click-clack go the elevator doors.
Leopards roam the streets, purring at the smell of gasoline.
Words whirl in storms, they are flown like kites by the urchin
velvet-suited children. The words are full of meaning; the children
   cheer.
Click-clack go the pistols of the police, coming to keep the poor
   hungry.
But there is light breaking out from the queen's tomb. You wander
   here,
and when I shake the globe, your pinched face fights against the waft
   of snow.

The Mouth of the River Grief

At the onset of the king-spindly feeling
my mouth grew numb and no longer spoke the sounds of the sea
in the rush of night
the feeling returned and I had a trembling in my knees and calves
all sense went out of my head
and I babbled like a sheep
my toes twisted themselves into roses' heads
and my tongue licked the sweat off my lips
in my belly the juices went dry
and I felt sick as old chips
the feeling ran through my veins
and I could no longer see or smell
faint music pulsed in juddering rhythms at the edge of the red sky
and my eyelids flickered in feather flight
at the height of the feeling the button was pushed
I fell into a hole that ate me up
soil teeth mulching
till I felt everything and nothing

Melancholia

I walk in green fields,
caught between the day and the night,
picking stars like September blackberries,
fighting blackness.

This purplish light spreads like a bruise
and in the gloom
the trees grow souls and speak to me.
They say:
Do not let the light in.
Live like stars in the dark.

Walk with my Father

The moment my cap flew off
and the bee stung my nose
and the red shoes left by the side of the road started walking off
and the wind rose into frenzy
and the bricks turned grey
and the trees laughed
and my shoelaces untied themselves
and my ankles hurt
but you made me carry on walking
and the people drinking Turkish coffee turned and stared
and the sun was weak
and the pavement cracks swallowed my face
that was the moment I realised you were not God

The Crows at Chatressac

You are sunk black.
Black scratches,
Thin bones feathered unkindly.

You eat light,
Fly into it with revulsion.

You make a noise like time-travel,
Nibble at rebels for breakfast.

This is a bleak picture,
Coarse pepper scattered across the sky.

Soot speckled peach.
Ants on a blushing cheek.

Quick as feet.
Sharp as flint.

Lifting like a Times Square elevator
Into a bony wind.
Caw, caw
With black beak
Which picks at scraps of ligament hungrily
Leaving mess.

If you turn on me I will hide and my shadow will tussle with you.
When you fly in clusters
Out of the tree by my window on a cold October morning,
I'll try not to throw plum stones at you.

Hell's Angels

A gun is a gun is a gun.

Melt gold and silver till the damn thing is gone.

The Cat King

The way that the light hits your face
when the April sun stuns and shifts,
a gathering of cherry blossom
present and implacable as water.
You look down at the unhurried pavement
with a flinch, as our cat crosses it

This cat, you say, and stop to stroke my cheek, I feel it.
A wind blows the cherry blossom across my face
into the conifer which shivers over the pavement,
and the cloud above shifts,
our cat is on the porch, sniffing at the drain water
and there is no other place I'd rather be than here, by the
    cherry blossom

With you and him, the Cat King, underneath the cherry blossom
searching for the meaning in all of it,
searching for the sun in the water
and the hidden look of approval in your face,
searching for the meaning in the shifts
of our moods, searching for the grouting in the pavement

as if the sun held the Cat King in its arms as he crossed the pavement
in this April dream, where you and I lie under cherry blossom,
until nothing is present but the shifts
of our moods, and in the heat of the day there's nothing but it,
as you and I map, with a finger, each other's face,
and when the sun is so high there's no trace of water.

The Cat King appears in the house, where we lie protracted
    like water,
the April skies shuddering down on the pavement,
our hands and eyes tracing each other's face
in the shade of the wind and cherry blossom
all of the shadows crossing the ground, lit
by the sun as it shifts

across the pavement, and in your arms, I smooth and shift
back into my April dream, with water
pouring down outside. Is it not anything but this, the shape of it?
The cherry blossom wilts and swirls in laps of pink gold on the
    pavement
and it builds till all I can feel is cherry blossom
and your eyes on my face,

but then the Cat King comes inside kissing my face,
and I awake, with him, the cherry blossom has fallen onto the
    pavement
irrevocably, and my cheeks are lit with water, for I have nothing but
    sorrow, the scent of it.

Lay All Your Love on Me

It may all be wasted emotion – a mote in the eye
but darling lay all your love on me   your fingers between my legs
this place lays bare my clouded dreams
it is so hot I would like to wash with milk but you –
soft as dust   glittered cheeks   old paper
the smell of books and the taste of ash
would you cook veal for me?
I am sitting in the empty kitchen in my underwear
waiting for the main course   and you walk in
your head held like a princely horse
it is so warm in your arms   I should like to die here

Young

A thousand doors ago
when I was a lonely kid
the stars hung from my window
and the spores of strangeness trailed in
there was no speech
nothing tangible as a word
and the moon saw and she shone
over my dark head
and she was my benefactor

The window bright at 2am
while I worked in my yellow notebook
not a dog awake
to keep me company
just the white moon
and her companions

It was a solitary fight
and I could have died right there
on the floor next to my bed
while everyone slept

The moon was impervious
though she drove off the darkness
with a great white push
and the yellow book glowed too
till the room was filled with light
and my dark head sang

Lebowski

I

He lifts a paw and taps me on the knee again and again, snagging on my tights with clipped claws. Scoop him up, he fits in the crook of my elbow like cold butter slowly melting. He smells of singed static, hot and needed as baby wipe, antiseptic, lithium. I watch him run along the garden wall, back legs white splash, his nose to wind. A knot in my heart, black fur bondage as real as oil. My love is cat-shaped, he is mine.

II

Ecstasy he makes, his noises. *Brroo-pip, rroaow, yeeaow, mii.* The purring deep in his ruffle chest, against my body warm as a photocopier: *hrrrrrrrrrrrrrrrrrrrrrr.* And suddenly: *Woo-hi-hi haow*, a message from outer space. His sneezes my love sonnets. *Hoorrrrrrhoorrrrrrr* all night again, my divine mix-tape. *Crunch, crunch, slurp*; the food I provide not nearly the sum of the love he gives.

III

When he miaows my ribs contract and I feel his little breath in my belly. When I watch him eat, I want to cry it's so beautiful. He is my animal. More. My creature come to comfort me, my confidant, my endless boundless fur-bound love, my sun-streaked white paw family. His small claws hook around my hand when I stroke his pale tummy in bed and I am complete. We are two animals sleeping, he and I, our breathing regular, the end of his tail a feather in my mouth.

IV

This cat, he is not a regular cat. He is eyes wide as sherbet saucers, black glass fur. The highlights around his pink nose, on his throat, and underneath his lean frame, lightning white. Ears, antennae for dubious sound, pricked up like an olive pierced on a stick and put to mouth. I cannot tell how much this cat knows me. I cannot say how he is of the earth and of the sky, studded cloud in his paw and hailstorm in his pattering legs. His tail is sometimes curled under his body for safekeeping, like a pearl earring in a trinket box.

Birthday on Rosewood Ward

The thin white sheet has come un-bunched and crumples under me. Scratchy blue blanket sags under my chin. I open my eyes, go into the main area in my NHS pyjamas, and see Nurse Barry with his laconic face. It cheers me. Yesterday he helped me clean up when I was sick in the hallway, from the smell.

It's my birthday I announce, to no one at large. Power Energy Sonia runs up to me and smiles, *I got you a present she says*, and hands it to me, unwrapped. It is earrings, pale yellow painted metal discs with a criss-crossed pattern and triangular studs. *Thank you* I say, and hug her tightly.

The curtains in my room are dusty from chalk pastel that I have been using to make endless drawings. I put the earrings in a cardboard box I'm using for jewellery. A torn photo of my cat is stuck onto the cracked mirror with dirty Blu Tack. I haven't seen him in three months, but soon I'm going home. All of a sudden it feels like my birthday.

Journeying North

Along the highway stand vats the size of giants' boots
electric pylons reaching for the moon
bats flitting homewards

we drive quietly and I think –
a grey dusk is as bad as sleepless dawn

the day a river of sighs
the night cold

and the text ticks on in the mind
in the end there
will be no beginnings

ACKNOWLEDGEMENTS

Some of these poems have been published in various online and print magazines and anthologies, thanks go to the editors of those:

Magma, Ink, Sweat and Tears, Rising, Blue of Noon, Tentacular, Strix, Goldfish, Shooter Literary Magazine, Anomalie, The Oxford Magazine, Holdfast Anthology, The Dizziness of Freedom Anthology (Bad Betty Press), *Alter Egos Anthology* (Bad Betty Press), *Witches, Warriors and Workers* (Culture Matters). 'Three Short Poems for Music' was commended in the Winchester Prize 2018, and 'Summer at St Pancras Hospital' was commended in the Winchester Prize 2020.

I am indebted to my many wonderful teachers and mentors: Matthew Caley, Sasha Dugdale, Mark Waldron, Vahni Capildeo, Julia Webb, Nick Drake, Maura Dooley, Daljit Nagra, Blake Morrison, Pascale Petit, Juliet Dusinberre and Anne Fernihough.

I am hugely grateful to Stuart Bartholomew and all at Verve Poetry Press for making it happen.

Heartfelt thanks also to my friends and colleagues who have supported me with feedback over the years: Jo Davis, Tom Bland, David McGrath, Melissa Lee Houghton, Serge Neptune, Lucy Walker, everyone in my Poetry School classes and Valeria's salon members.

Huge thanks to Oliver Weindling and all at the Vortex Jazz Club, and to Aurelie Freoua for inspiration and support.

To my brilliant friends, love and thanks for everything.

And to my family, my rock: Jacqueline Ross, Ulrich Heinen, Bruno Heinen, Noemi Caruso, Anita Caruso Heinen, Elise Ross, Eliot Rattle, Sacha Rattle, Zeynep Oszuca, Luca Finn Rattle, Elaine Heinen, Anna Heinen, Jamshid Amiry and Benedict Heinen, thanks and love always.

ABOUT VERVE POETRY PRESS

Verve Poetry Press is a quite new and already award-winning press that focused initially on meeting a local need in Birmingham - a need for the vibrant poetry scene here in Brum to find a way to present itself to the poetry world via publication. Co-founded by Stuart Bartholomew and Amerah Saleh, it now publishes poets from all corners of the UK - poets that speak to the city's varied and energetic qualities and will contribute to its many poetic stories.

Added to this is a colourful pamphlet series, many featuring poets who have performed at our sister festival - and a poetry show series which captures the magic of longer poetry performance pieces by festival alumni such as Polarbear, Matt Abbott and Geraldine Carver.

In 2019 the press was voted Most Innovative Publisher at the Saboteur Awards, and won the Publisher's Award for Poetry Pamphlets at the Michael Marks Awards.

Like the festival, we strive to think about poetry in inclusive ways and embrace the multiplicity of approaches towards this glorious art.

www.vervepoetrypress.com
@VervePoetryPres
mail@vervepoetrypress.com

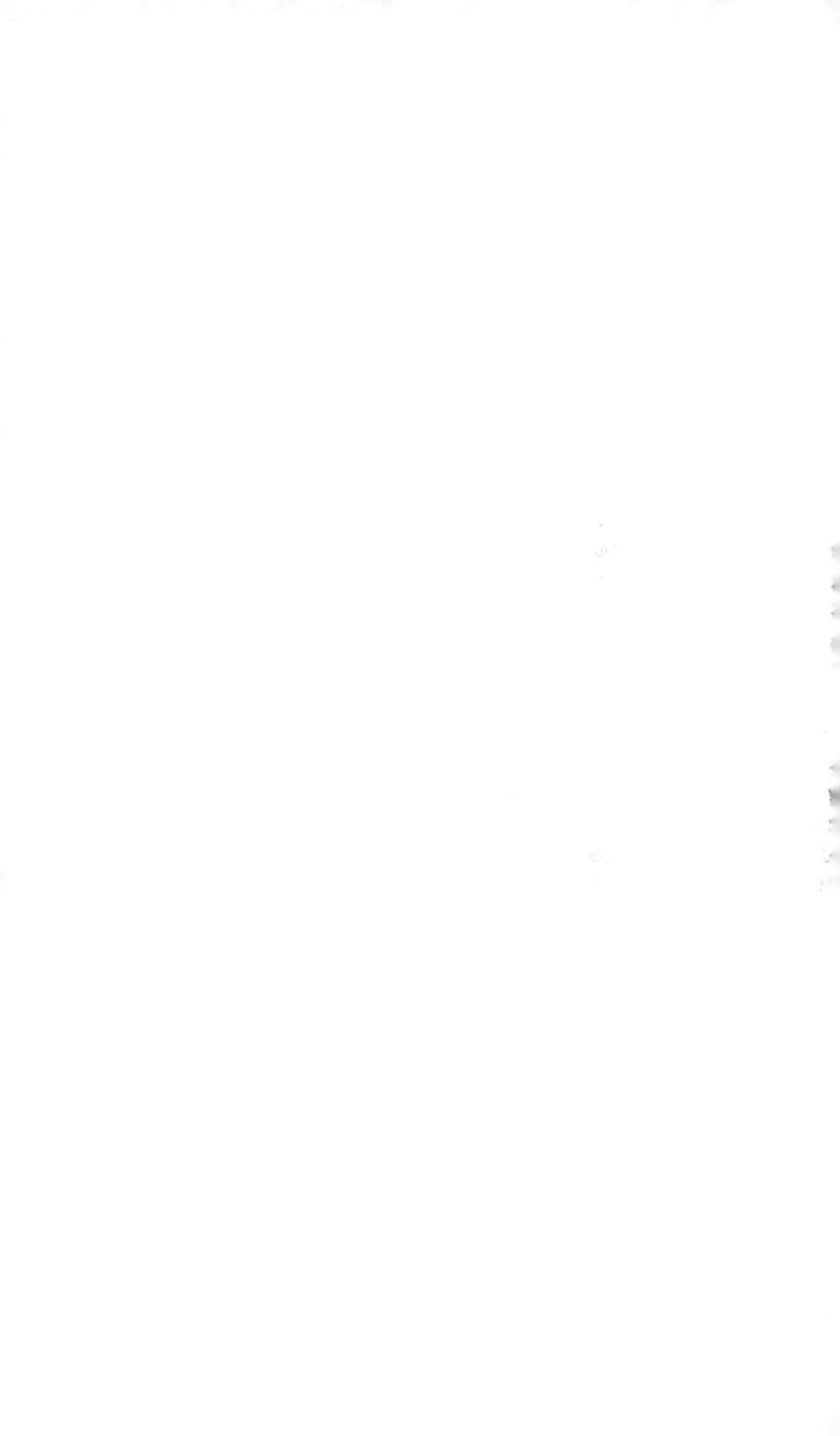